HOPE IN HOPELESSNESS

Contents

Fun. Wild. Crazy. Loving. Outgoing. 'Never had a care in the world'. Deanna Hanger. Trying to kill myself in my twenties proved one thing. I lost each and every one of those qualities. Gone. Vanished. Done. If you told me 15 years ago that I would survive mental illnesses, I would not have believed you. My life was a smooth record playing the sweetest of songs crooning Mozart, until an ugly scratching noice replaced everything I knew. My life was in hell...

Clinical depression, obsessive-compulsive thoughts, anxiety, dissociative disorder. Letting you into my head at this critical tine in my life is vulnerable. Letting you into the battle of my everyday life is bold. Vulnerability. We need more of it.

The battle to live. Could I live each day through hell for the rest of my life? This is the question I struggled with every single second. My life was was on a thread. Deciding if my life was worth living was the ultimate question. To cut the thread or not was the ultimate decision. It's always the people you least expect who deal with such horrible things. These are the people who hide what they are going through. They put on a mask and pretend that everything is fine.

This way of thinking is BULLSHIT . It's okay to say you're not okay! It's okay to say you're struggling! That living life is way too much to bear. There is hope in everything. Literally everything, no matter how much your situation tells you differently.

What is this book about, you ask? It's real life! Real notes I took while going through depression... AKA Pure Torturous Hell. Sounds a little dramatic, right? Nope. Those words don't even shine a light on the pain of all those years. I want to tell you what I've learned and what needs to be known by those who are struggling, even those who have misconceptions about mental illnesses. I want to be one hundred percent real.

We've done a good job giving the wrong answers. Every time we hear about someone who has mental illnesses, we treat them like they need to get over it and snap out of it. This is all untrue and it needs to be set straight. This book is for anyone and everyone. Mental illness does not care what race, ethnicity, religion, status you are; it can hit anyone. Anytime.

I'm going to warn you: the things I wrote as I was going through depression were all negative and ultimately lies. I never realized they were lies until I beat depression and could open my eyes up again. While I was depressed, I saw these lies as truth. It took the help of my friends and therapy to set me straight and find truth in my life. They told me, 'Deanna, you're going to get through this. There is a light at the end of the tunnel. Killing yourself is not the way out. It's not the answer to any of this.' No matter how many times they told me this, I truly believed that killing myself was the one and only answer. I felt that it was the only logical decision I had. I thought it would end all my pain. There would be no more hurting, no more living, no more anything. It all sounded so good and final that it had to be the only answer. But, after breaking out of depression, I have to admit, it was a lie. It was a horrible, wicked, no good, ugly lie that consumes so many people. It breaks my heart.

01
LETTER-

Five years ago, I would never have thought I would be writing this letter. I'm not going to give reasons as to why I killed myself. Instead, I want you to remember the good Deanna. What happened to that Deanna, I cannot give an answer. I do know that she is gone and is never coming back. If this is a mental illness I give it props. People have always told me throughout my life I am a strong person. I guess this just proves how much this has taken a toll on me. I cannot continue life living like this. No matter how many times someone tells me it's not going to last forever, they do not know what my situation is. I don't even know what to call it. I will not continue living like this.

I have grown to know what really causes suicide —hopelessness. It is the very sense that there is no hope and there will never be an any hope. No way out. No changing back to 'normal.'

I don't want this to just be another one of those suicide notes that say, 'I am sorry', and continue with, 'I love you, mom and dad, friends and family.' I don't even want this note to be considered a suicide note. Instead, it is a note that finally expresses why things were too much for me to handle. It is time to do something about it. I have to end the situation. Unfortunately, this means taking my life. There is no other way out. I wish I had a little more energy in me like before. I don't want you to remember the sad, angry, depressed, anxiety- filled, troubled person I have been for the past few years.

Life is funny. One moment, it can be going at an incredibly, fun, exhilarating rate. All of a sudden, it crashes and burns. You're left speechless. I wish I could have held on a little longer.

God knows my heart and I hope I do, too. I miss loving life. I miss making people laugh and smile in my presence. I miss having people wanting to hang out with me . I miss my personality. The way I used to see life, it was beautiful. I saw beauty in the little things. I am so thankful to God for giving me a good 18 years. I loved and enjoyed those years to the fullest. I am no longer angry. No longer sad. Just empty and wanting an end to everything.

I love every single one of you and I wish you the best of luck in this crazy thing we all call life. Please remember me for who I once was, because that person? That person was great. Unfortunately, this is my time. It's the end for me. I hope I affected many people for the good, because this was my goal. I wanted to use my humor to help people who were having a bad day . I wanted to be there for people who were struggling. I really wanted to just be the best version of myself I could be. I hope I achieved this for at least some of you. I love you. I do not have the motivation to get up and do things anymore. I really hope this death came as a surprise to most of you. I hope that I covered up what I was going through as much as possible, because it sure did take a lot out of me to pretend. You have taught me love and what it means to have a good time in life.

I know I keep on saying goodbye and then writing more. I don't want to say goodbye to you guys and ultimately, to life. I feel like I have to end it because it's all over. The way I used to live has been destroyed. I'm sorry you have to hear that, but it's the truth. You ought to have an explanation for this. I am so ashamed of taking my own life because I know deep down that life is a gift. I know deep down I love life so much. I wish I didn't have to cut it this short or even cut it at all. There was so much for me to learn, grow, and expound on. I had such high hopes of having a future and growing up.

I wish I was better, so I could have more memories. I think that's why we need good memories. God sure knew we need them just to get through the bad days. Right now, I am remembering all the good things instead of the bad. If only I could live like this every day. I cannot go back to living the life I loved. I cannot love like I used to. I cannot do ANYTHING like I used to, and this is what upsets me the most. I know it will last my whole life. I hate living 2 seconds like this. This is why I need to kill myself and end this nonsense. I am so sorry for those who will get hurt. I promise you, I am sorry.

02

OKAY-

Watching a movie, doing homework, hanging out, joking around, anything I do is saying I am okay when I really am not. I feel fake. I feel as if I am lying to myself. Doing normal things whether it be grocery shopping or therapy, it's all saying, 'I'm okay,' but it is far from the truth. I am forced to be "okay." I don't want to do any of these things.It's stupid, horrible, and so frustrating. I might have some good days, but that doesn't mean I am doing well. I feel that in order to be fine, something in me needs to detach. I feel like a plague or a curse is on me. I know that's not what it is, but that's the only way I can describe it.

Summary: As I was writing this, I remember thinking to myself, nothing about me was 'okay.' That thought was intense. Any activity, whether it be brushing my teeth, going to the movies, or going to work, felt that I was saying, 'I am good,' since I was still doing those things. When you go through something as intense as a mental illness, the tendency is to hide it right away. You don't want anyone to know there is something 'wrong' with you. You want to make an impression that you are still ' normal.' But really... What is normal? We still haven't figured it out; nobody has it figured out. We are human, and that means we don't have it all figured out. We are flawed. Nobody on the planet is perfect. Everyone goes through something hard. Huge or small, we are bound to have something happen to us. That is one thing life guarantees for us. If we started living and realizing that everyone is going through this thing called life together, if we started telling ourselves that nobody is perfect, we would be able to relate to each other more and stop feeling the need to be fake. Being real to people is the best thing we can do! Yes, it takes a lot of courage and vulnerability to be real. But that's way better than feeling like I am living a lie.

I knew I wasn't okay, but everyone else thought I was because from the outside, I was the same as always. It took a lot of effort for me to pretend to be my normal self— the Deanna Hanger that everyone knew and loved. I didn't know that my friends and family could still love and accept me even if they knew what I was going through. That effort of acting was tiresome and took a lot out of me. It burned me out. I wasn't able to regain any happiness until I stopped bottling my feelings and thoughts and pretending I needed to have it all together.

03

FEELING-

I play it up and try to be my old self. It's hard to keep trying to be yourself when you know that you are not you anymore. How is it even possible to not know how to be yourself? I could clearly see the difference between who I was back then and who I am now. Am I even a person? Am I still a human being? I lie in bed completely emotionless for hours, just staring at a wall. Emotionally dead.

Summary: Before all this I was filled with joy. I lived for the fun of life. I went from loving life to being emotionless. Mental illnesses can rob you of who you were and turn you into someone unrecognizable. I didn't know who I was anymore. I didn't feel like I was a person. My illnesses took the life out of me and changed who I was—made me into a person I didn't know or want to know.

I had to look at my keepsakes and old photo albums to remember who I was and to remind myself that I had a life before all this hell. It helped me remember that I was still human. I remember looking into a mirror one night, crying, tearing my hair out, and feeling that the person I was staring at was not me. I had no connection to that person. I would feel like I was literally escaping from my body because I could not handle everything going on internally. Unfortunately, this is a normal thing for people who suffer from dissociation.

One instance has always lingered in my mind that portrays this concept so perfectly. One day, I was in the kitchen when my mom cut her hand with a knife accidentally while cooking. The cut was deep and needed stitches. She needed to be taken to the hospital. I felt no sympathy or even the slightest pinch of sadness that she was in pain. I just stared at her while thinking about my emotional pain and how I couldn't take her to the hospital. Numbness like this is the worst feeling in the world: not feeling anything anymore, just remembering how you used to feel. But I will tell you this: hitting rock bottom like this emotionally has given me a different perspective I didn't think was possible. I took for granted the ability to just feel. Emotions and feelings are a gift! I now have more respect for life. Transformation took place inside me through these long years, transformation that could only come from hitting the lowest of all lows. A life long transformation I never would have believed. I am a firm believer when you hit the lowest of lows the only place you can go from there is up.

04

THOUGHTS-

Something is not right. Life feels weird. Why can't it be as simple as not having this feeling? My mind works every second against me. There is never a time I'm not constantly in my head. I'm hurting, I'm hurting, and I'm hurting. I know something is wrong. I feel it. At what point does this end? At what point do I get to say this is done, it's over? When can I have a say in anything at all? Do I have to kill myself? Do I need to keep crying and pulling my hair out in torment? Will this ever be over?

Summary: Something *was* wrong, and it was called OCD. When you have obsessive- compulsive disorder, you get unwanted and intrusive thoughts that are on repeat in your head. Thoughts you do not want, skipping over and over and over again. They never stop. I was so consumed by my thoughts that I had to sleep as much as possible just to get out of my head for a couple of hours. If you know someone who is going through this, just know it is not their fault or their choice to be stuck. They can't escape it no matter how hard they try. Just being there for them until they find something to help ease their thoughts is the best thing you can possibly do for them. Being there for someone with OCD can be very hard and tiring, but don't give up!

05

RELATE-

You don't know what it's like to have your own mind working against you. If you were to have it just for a day, you would understand. If only you knew what goes on inside of me daily. I can't handle this by myself. This is too much for someone to deal with alone.

Summary: Often I thought, "If only people knew what was happening to me/ inside me." There is a powerful truth to that thought. If someone has a mental illness and their friends and family have never dealt with such a thing, they simply cannot relate. It feels like torture to have the people you care most about not know anything about what is going on. What I went through was horrible. It was inexplicable to me. No matter how hard I tried to tell people what was going on, it didn't matter because they would give me surface level information. I couldn't apply any of it to my life. Don't get me wrong, these people I reached out to loved me and wanted the best for me. They truly cared; they just did not know how to help or how to relate. It wasn't until I opened up to my best friend, who went through similar situations, that I got the help I needed. I expected her to give me an answer for ending the pain, but she didn't. She actually told me quite often how she didn't have the answer. Her telling me that I was not crazy, was everything. She told me she remembered having similar feelings that I was experiencing. What it comes down to is being connected on a human being level.

The last therapist I went to was my rock. She had been in practice for thirty years. I opened up to her and she didn't judge me. She gave me useful tips that I could use in my life. She told me that I was not alone, that I was not the only one going through this. This lifted a huge weight off my shoulders because so often, I believed that I was the only one enduring this type of pain.

I believed that no one could relate to me and no one understood. This was a powerful lie. It's a lie that takes people's lives away. If you don't know any friends or family and you can't find a therapist you like, then find a support group. Yes, I know that sounds stupid and dumb, but it's not. As human beings, we were created to be around people. We aren't meant to be isolated. We need to have someone to relate to in hard times, whether we are facing financial problems, marital problems, or sickness. If we can find people to talk to, people who can relate, it makes a world of a difference. Isolation is the worst thing we can possibly do.

06

ESCAPE-

The mountains; they are amazing. I can just be here and not care about anything. I can stare at them forever. There is peace here and somehow it calms my soul. There is no pressure, whatsoever, for anything. I don't have to keep them entertained or make them like me. They don't care. The mountains are just there. I can sit and stare at them as long as I want to. In times when I have nowhere else to go and I don't want to see anyone, they are a safe haven. They are a place to go when I am troubled and want to be calmed.

Summary: It is so very important to find your escape. Let me re-phrase that. A healthy escape. There has to be something or somewhere you can find peace and tranquility. You need a place to escape from everything going on inside and around you. It can be going out into nature, cooking, watching movies, surfing, anything that makes you feel at peace. Find it. Everyone is going to have a different way of escaping, and that's the beauty of it.We are all different. Finding a healthy way to escape the chaos is a huge step towards healing.

I don't want you to cope with cutting yourself, taking drugs, or drinking alcohol. You are just numbing the pain. It might go away temporarily, but I guarantee you, you will feel the same as before.

In my case, I felt so numb and so unmotivated that even thinking about watching a movie was too much effort for me. I couldn't do it. But, there was something about nature and the mountains that gave me the motivation to go. I felt so much peace. The mountains were a place I could keep on writing until all my thoughts ran out. The mountains were my safe place.

07 MATTERS-

No one should have to go through this. No one should go to the mountains alone in their car with their knees to their chest, skinny because they lost 30 pounds, hunched over and staring out of the car, crying for three hours. I have a story that needs to be heard. If I ever get better, I will fight for this story to be heard. After going through hell and back, I will not start again and act as if nothing happened. Things happened and I need to do something with it. I will make it known to those hurting and struggling for help and hope. I vow that.

Summary: I remember this night so vividly. I remember crying so much that I didn't think it was possible to cry any more. But, the tears just kept coming. It lasted for hours.

If you are thinking about killing yourself or ending the situation, you need to know and believe this: your life matters. Let me repeat that—your life matters. You, yes you. You need to know you are valued and loved. Your life matters!!! I cannot stress that enough. This is the truth. I don't care about all the past mistakes, the decisions you have made, I am telling you right now that you matter no matter what and you can make a difference in the world. What are your passions? Follow them! Do what you love. Write a book about what you have been through. Be the first one to make it to another planet. Be the best singer in the world. You matter. Always.

08

THOUGHTS-

What am I doing? Seriously, what am I doing right now? I can't stay in the mountains forever. I definitely can't stay here until I am 90 years old. I don't want to go down there. I don't want to go back to civilization. I don't want to be around people. I don't want to do anything that the world considers normal. So, what do I do? There is nothing else left. It's one or the other, and I hate them both. I'm always contradicting myself. If I go down there and continue with the normal things I'm expected to do, I will not be happy.

AIII want to do is fix this. I want to press a button and make this all go away. I want everything to go back to normal. This mental illness has torn me up, destroyed me, and spit me out. It's insane. In a sense, it has killed me from the inside. I can't believe all this is just because of my brain. I am living in hell, every single slow second. I am dead inside, yet I'm still alive on the outside.

I don't want tomorrow to come. I don't want it to be a new day. It's not even about me struggling to get through the day anymore.

It's more than that, but I don't know how to write it in words. It's unreal. This is not happening; life isn't happening. I want to put some sense back into something that does not and cannot make sense.

I do know one thing I am thankful for. I am thankful for when I am alone in the mountains. Silence. There is nothing but beauty. Here, I can write all these things down. I don't want to pretend anymore. I am tired of pretending, but I have to because if I don't, I will never see people. I will never come out of my room. I will be torn up and thrown out of the world because that's how it works. Life is hard and if you lag behind your done. Game over. Move to the back because there are better people out there who will gladly take your spot. The world is ruthless. It keeps on going even when you want it to stop.

I don't know what I want. I don't even know if I want to heal anymore. I'm tired of knowing I'm not okay and continuing that way. I hate being forced to be okay. This is horrible. Living is just acting. It is acting like you're okay even when you're not. Stop and really think about how powerful that is. Living is acting like you're okay. Wow.

Summary: If there is one thing I want to stress, it's that you will hear lies while going through depression and mental illness. There will be so many lies that they will drown out the truth. There will be so much negativity that you cannot see anything positive. I became so contradictory and I felt so out of this world that I couldn't even tell if I was a person. Powerful, right? The mind is powerful. But just like any muscle in your body, you can actually train it. You can train your mind to think the thoughts you want it to. You can start to believe the things you tell your mind. When you say you can't do it, you won't do it. You will believe you cannot.

I remember how my thoughts would contradict almost everything. For example, when a friend would tell me how I needed to get out of bed and hang out with people, I would say, "Yes I will go out." Ten minutes later, I would say, "Actually, I don't think I'm going to go." I would go back and forth for thirty minutes. The thoughts in my mind were saying, "I don't want to go out. I know I should and it will be good for me. I don't want to be around people. But at the same time, I do want to be around people." I actually didn't want anything. I didn't want to be around people, but I also wanted to be around people at the same time. Doesn't make sense, huh? My thoughts would always contradict. They didn't make any sense. I was confused about life, about the simplest things. Everything stopped making sense. It was almost as if my life was two negative poles of two magnets trying to come together. It never would. In theory, depression makes sense. But, when you actually have it and are going through it, it's inexplicable.

09

TIME-

You know that saying, "Take one step at a time: one foot in front of the other"? That's literally what you have to do. You can't look at the future. You can't even look at tomorrow. Right now means just worrying about right now.

I hate doctors appointments. I can't think of having a lazy couple of days, eating breakfast at my house, or hanging out with friends. I hate thinking that far in advance. I don't want to live another day. I don't want to be myself. I want to die. Why can't I just say I'm over it... Why can't this just disappear?

Summary: Time is an interesting concept. We are held down to it. It's the way things were made and designed. Time can be a good thing, but time can also work against us. After going through hell and back, I understood that time was the hardest thing surrounding me. I was told about a light at the end of the tunnel, but I wanted that tunnel right now. There was no waiting for me. I was in such a critical condition that it was only a matter of time before I would kill myself and end it all.

This is when you have to train your mind to realize that you can only take time by each second. Each moment. You cannot look ahead of yourself in the future because all you will see is hopelessness. You cannot see the light at the end of the tunnel because you are currently in the tunnel and the tunnel is very dark. Taking it moment by moment, second by second, allows you to get through each day. Often, it even seems impossible to even do that. The good thing about time and going through what I went through is that it made me a stronger person. Time can work against you, but it can also work for you in the end.

10

UNNAMABLE-

It's hard to say I am going to be okay. It's hard to say I am going to get through this. I don't even know what *this* is and what it will take to fix it. Music is good, though. Music soothes and calms my soul.

I want to be new again. I want to be alive again. Right now I feel dead. I am just walking around aimlessly because I have to. I want to be how I used to be. It seems like this isn't even real life, but it is. Show me where I went wrong; show me what happened to my life! Give me anything, I am desperate. What is going on?

Summary: What you're going through is unnamable if you don't know the science behind it and what's happening in your brain. For the first two years, I didn't know I had depression, OCD, and anxiety. I thought something was just wrong with me. I thought maybe I screwed up and was going through hell because of it. I thought whatever I was going through was unnamable. I had no idea a mental illness was causing everything. It wasn't until I went to clinics when I understood it all. My brain scan gave me proof of what exactly my brain was doing. Mental illnesses are a brain problem. Your brain has chemicals in it that need to be balanced. If they are unbalanced, it can cause hell. My unbalanced brain affected me physically, emotionally, and spiritually. In a sense, it affected everything about me. It wasn't until I started taking medication that everything went back to normal. Medication made the parts that were overworking and the parts that were underworking equal out. It wasn't until my brain chemicals were balanced that my life balanced out as well, leading me to become more emotionally stable.

11

NOTHING-

I have nothing left to make me want to get better. I don't know what to do anymore. I lost my willpower to fight. Asking someone who wishes to kill himself to keep on going every day. This is insane. Why must I keep on going? Why is death so final? I don't want to keep on going. I don't want to do anything. I don't even know what to say anymore. I am tired of writing my feelings, because they never end. They're always the same.

Summary: Coming to the end of your life is scary. It's scary to think that there is nothing out there to heal you or take away your pain. Seeing and thinking of death as the only answer is a terrifying place to be. It's a very sobering thought. I came to a point where I had nothing left inside me to keep fighting. In fact, that was exactly what I was doing: I was fighting for my life. This is going to be a hard concept for those who have never had depression or can't relate to any mental illness. But to those who have come to this point, I know what it feels like. You're not alone. You are not a bad person for wanting to end your misery. You need to know there are other ways to get out of this, though. Killing yourself is not the answer, nor will it ever be.

I knew death was final and it scared me that once I made that decision, there was no coming back. It was the end of it all. As scared as I was and as sobering as that thought was, anything was better than living another second the way I was. If you see things this way, you need to find someone to tell this to right now. Every time I tried or attempted to end it all, I would call my friend. Deep, deep inside me, I knew death was not what I wanted. I didn't want it to be the end forever. I just wanted my *situation* to end forever.

Wanting to end your situation by killing yourself is not the solution. I don't believe this is what you really want, either. I think you cry when you think of dying and your tears are a reminder that you don't want it to end. Listen to your tears. Let them guide your heart in finding another way of ending this misery. Find a way that is not as final as death. Find something that doesn't hurt you physically.

12

HATE-

hate myself for going. I hate myself for not going. This is taking me away and changing me into a different person, but not in a good way. Everything feels like the biggest deal in the world because everything is magnified. I want to go hang out, but a heavy sleepiness came over me. None of this makes sense. It always contradicts and ruins everything— plans, relationships, me. I hate depression and OCD. But, I won't kill myself because of depression. I am stronger than that.

Summary: I hated myself so much. I didn't realize that this mental illness was making me this way. It wasn't as if I was choosing to be like this, but I didn't get that at the time. I thought I made myself that way. Don't let this illness get away with that thought. This is not you, and it does not give you the permission to hate yourself. This is not your choice. If this was your choosing, you would have already healed from this. I remember wanting to press a button that would make everything normal again. Learn how to love yourself through this. You owe yourself that. I didn't do that, but if I did, it would have made things just a little bit easier. Instead, I ended up hating myself throughout everything.

13

WISHING-

I don't want to do this anymore. Please take my life, God, please— I am crying out to you. Just please take my life. It was not my choice to be put on this earth.

Summary: I remember wishing for a lot of things. I remember wishing I was dead, wishing God would kill me naturally so I didn't have to kill myself. Wishing I was never born, and wishing God wasn't real. These things I wished for were what I was feeling.

Tell God what you're feeling. Tell Him you hate Him for what you're going through, tell Him you are having doubts if He is even real. He is not intimated by your thoughts or wishes. He is above them, and He has conquered them all. You may waver through your emotions and thoughts, but He never does. Many things change around us. Friends come and go; you may find a different job. Change is inevitable. Knowing God's character never changes is so comforting.

14

DREAM-

I will get through this.

Summary: There were times when I told myself I needed to be stronger and I had to proclaim the truth. Doing this didn't change my situation, but it helped me feel more at peace with myself. Proclaim the truth instead of the lies that your mental illness is telling you.

I learned to speak the truth into my situation because if I didn't, the lies would have overpowered and drowned me. I would have started to believe the lies being whispered in my ear.

15

QUESTIONS-

Where do I get the strength to keep going? It's overwhelming and unbearable. I cannot live life with this. I can't do anything about this. Who cares about anything when I am like this? How can an individual handle this all? It's impossible to even talk to a therapist about things. I hope this is a mental illness because I can't live with myself if this turns out to just be me. I'm physically and emotionally beat. There is pain inside me. I don't know where it's from or what it all is. All I can say is I feel physical pain inside me right now. I am so tired of everything. I don't know what to do. Nobody can do anything for me, not even myself.

Three years without peace. I just want one second of rest. I want all this taken away. I want to know what happened and why so much has been taken away from me. I might seem okay on the outside but I'm far from okay. I am 20 years old. I should be dealing with things like dating, school, etc. I can't live like this. What have I done?

I am empty. I am hurting inside so much that I can actually feel physical pain in my heart. I have breakdowns in the shower trying to figure out what I did wrong. I cannot do this on my own. None of this makes sense. What can possibly happen to change this? What a waste of life. What happens when things become too much? What happens when you want to die? I don't know what to do anymore. I've lost my willpower to fight. Asking someone who wants to die to keep on going and not giving them any answers. I don't even know what to say anymore; I am tired of writing my feelings down because they never end and they're always the same.

Summary: There are going to be a lot of questions and you will want answers to them now. This applies to everything: we want answers to the things that are unknown and foreign to us. Especially if it''s a critical time we're living in. It's uncomfortable being in the unknown without any answers. This is where trust is so important. Put your trust in friends, family, and mentors. Your thoughts will tell you lies. You need to overcome those lies by listening to people who are trying to speak truth into you. Put your faith in someone even when your mind is telling you not to.

16

LIFE-

What do I do? What is going on? What has happened to me? Why can't I laugh? Why do I only cry? Where have I gone? What do I do while living every day? Where do I go? Why can't I choose to get better right now? Why do I have to wait for years? Everything is always about not knowing. I'm gone and I am not myself. I have no personality. No more Deanna Hanger. It's over, everything is over. What happened? I wasn't always like this? I had a life before this. I didn't have to keep looking through keepsakes to remind myself of who I was. The person in the keepsakes has died.

I am trying to understand this. I am trying so hard, but the answer is hidden in a locked treasure chest somewhere. I have to go blindly through a maze to find this box, and in the end of this confusion I find out there is no treasure chest. That is what it is like. This is what it feels like to never be able to find an answer, not even a little one. Grasping, pleading, screaming for an answer, but there is nothing out there. That is why this is hopeless. There is no hope to be found no matter how many people tell you there is. It's all a lie. What do you do when your mind is working against itself? How are you supposed to not believe your mind? I don't want to hear it anymore. I am utterly confused and I am hating my life right now. I hate living like this every day. Actually, scratch that, I hate living every second like this. Am I supposed to be strong? I can't live another second if I have to live like this, and I don't want to. I almost killed myself.

What happened and what is going on? Why can't I live without this? Why can't I just have my life back? I want to get away but I can't.

Summary: I came to a point where I didn't want to be in myself anymore. I didn't want to be a person. I was so tired, weary, and burdened. I thought I was supposed to be strong. I thought I was supposed to do this on my own. I thought I needed to be happy all the time even though I wasn't. I dreaded life.

We are human. We were made to feel. But sometimes, people feel too much and it's hard. I'm telling you right now, we aren't created to always be happy. There are times when we are going to cry, scream out in anger, or be on top of the mountains. It is life. It's not always going to be easy. One person might be going through one thing and another person another thing, but we're all bound together thorough the messiness of life. The best part is, not a single person in the whole world has figured out life completely. It's the beauty of learning and growing.

17

NOW-

So many times, I have too much to say. I try to write them all down but I can't get the words for them. Eventually, I just stop and don't care, even though I really do care. It is easier to just numb the whole thing and stop.

Summary: I have written so many things about what I've learned after coming out from my depression and mental illnesses. But, you should take note of the keywords, "coming out of it." You cannot be numb forever. You have to find a healthy way out, and killing yourself is not the answer. My way of coming out was medication. I chose to balance my brain chemicals and be myself again. I chose to be a person again. The time is now. I promise you once you get out of depression, you will be a stronger person. But, the most important thing is to get out of it first. How do you get out of it? It's hard for me to tell you this, but I don't have ONE answer. But, that's only because everyone is different. I just know what I've gone through and what has helped me. You might be different. Maybe you just needed support to back you up and get you out of a funk. Maybe you just needed to feel loved. Maybe you do need to find the right medication or find a therapist to talk to and help you get through this time of your life. I am saying "time in your life" because no matter what or who you are, this is a time of your life. I, Deanna Hanger, am telling you right now that it is one hundred percent possible for you to get through this and get out of this torture. This is a temporary time of your life.

I do want to talk more about medication; it saved my life. Without it, I would not have been able to write this book. It wasn't a walk in the park, though. It took me two years to find the right medication. Everyone is different. We all have different brains, so there is not one medication that works for everyone. There are so many different kinds of medications. Some medications will work for you and others won't. I had many medications that made me worse. I hate and love medication because of this. When time is so vital and you're at a point where you're willing to take your life, it's hard to spend weeks trying out a medication. It's a long process, and some may not be able to wait for.

I got brain scans done and they told me what exact medications would work for my brain specifically. They told me something interesting for those who are wary about medication. When we have a broken leg or arm, we have it scanned to see what the problem is. Why is it any different for the brain when, in a sense, it is broken? But I will say this: medication isn't for everyone, I believe it should be the last resort. If you have other options, you can go take that route. But if it becomes unbearable, I would have an open mind to going on medication.

18
HOPE-

You don't understand. There is no hope. Everything else has hope except for this one thing. How is someone supposed to listen and understand me if I don't even understand myself? This is literally taking away all my joy and it's not fair. Am I just supposed to live life like this? It sucks because I have the day off tomorrow and I can't even just have fun. I don't want to do anything. There are times when none of this seems real. It's all so crazy and I don't get why I have to live like this. Why not someone else? Why can't I just have my life? Living like this hurts. I should be in my room all the time and not do anything and give up.

I am over this. I just want my life back. I want to be able to have the choice to live life again. I can't do this. I don't know what to do. I want to cry. I just want myself back. This isn't me. I'm tired of having this. I'm not okay with this. How can it take away all my joy? I used to love life. My happiness and joy are being stolen. This can't be real. I just want to cry for the rest of my life. Why am I even going to work? Why am I doing anything? What is keeping me going? It sucks that I can't die. I want to die. I can't do this. I can't do this. I can't do this.

Summary: I don't know why I kept going. I think it was the truth of really not wanting to die.I just wanted all the crap to end. The fact that I am living and writing this book now means you can do it. Have you ever heard of the saying, "If I can do it, you can too?" That is what I am going to tell you right now. You can do this, you can get through this, and you are capable. You can do this even if you don't have anything in you that wants to get better anymore. If you've lost your willpower to fight, live one second at a time and ask people to help you find an answer. There is hope in your situation. There is always hope. Hope is powerful. It can get you through anything. I went through a time when I didn't see any hope, and yet I am here today. There is hope for you and your life. There is hope for everyone.

19
CONCLUSION-

What have I learned through this all? So much. Mental illnesses tear you apart spiritually, physically, emotionally, and mentally. In a sense, they really are killing you second by second from the inside out. However, healing is possible. Possible through people—friends, family, people who love you. At first, when this depression started, I didn't tell anyone. I pretended I was okay. I was unable to be vulnerable to anyone about what I was going through. As time went on, I literally could not do it alone. I just kept on going.

I did seek out a lot of help, but nothing worked. I was looking for an answer, desperate for anything. No one had the answer I was looking for. But empathy was there for me from people going through the same thing. If I had not gone through any of this, I would be freaked out if someone told me they wanted to kill themselves. I would be weirded out if someone told me they couldn't live another second. I would, of course, have sympathy for their hurt. But, how could I ever help them as much as I want to now? I wouldn't be able to because really, if I was honest with myself, I wouldn't truly know what they were going through. But because I had depression, OCD, and everything else, I can relate to those who have the same thing. Going through this has given me more compassion towards people. It has given me more love, more patience, and more vulnerability. It has allowed me to be honest about everything.

I now have this desire to help those who are feeling helpless and hopeless. My friend went through similar things and I was able to talk to her. I was able to be honest with her. She understood and empathized with me. She was there for me when no one else really could be. She knew how to help, and help she did. She was there for me to talk about everything and anything. She was there for me, and I could cry in her arms for hours. I could call her on the phone and sometimes, I would cry multiple times a day. She was there for me when I tried to kill myself and she wouldn't let me hang up the phone until she got to my house. I'm telling you right now, if you are going through something, get a friend or a family member and tell them everything, no matter how hard it is to say the truth. Allow them go through this with you. You need at least one person to be in your life in your time of need. You cannot, and I repeat, cannot get through or out of this on your own, no matter how strong you are.

The last thing I want to leave you with is the word hope. Hope is powerful. I lived without hope for four years, and once I hit that spot of hopelessness and helplessness, there really wasn't much to live for. That's why I tried to kill myself. There was no reason in continuing life if my life was going to be like that forever. Why then should I not end the misery and torture right now, right? So many people would tell me about a light at the end of the tunnel. I've been told that it's not going to be like this forever, but I knew 100 percent it would. Nothing was going to change, and I was sure of it. But I was wrong. I will be the first to tell you that no matter how helpless your situation proves, there is ALWAYS hope. You can tell me, "Deanna, you don't understand, my situation is hopeless." My words to you would be, "There is hope." Hope will help you through.